# ASSESSING READING DIFFICULTIES

A diagnostic and remedial approach

LYNETTE BRADLEY

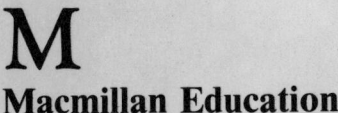
Macmillan Education

# Macmillan Education
# Tests and Assessment Advisory Board

Professor Jack Wrigley, Deputy Vice Chancellor,
University of Reading.
Bridie Raban, Department of Educational Studies,
Oxford University.
Dr Conrad Graham, Special Education Adviser.
Denis R. Vincent, Reader in Education, North
East London Polytechnic.

© Lynette Bradley 1980

All rights reserved. No reproduction, copy or transmission
of this publication may be made without written permission.

No paragraph of this publication may be reproduced, copied
or transmitted save with written permission or in accordance
with the provisions of the Copyright Act 1956 (as amended).

Any person who does any unauthorised act in relation to
this publication may be liable to criminal prosecution and
civil claims for damages.

First published 1980
Reprinted 1984, 1985

Published by
MACMILLAN EDUCATION LTD
Houndmills, Basingstoke, Hampshire RG21 2XS
and London
Companies and representatives
throughout the world

Printed in Hong Kong

ISBN 0-333-37916-0

# Contents

| | |
|---|---|
| **Preface** | iv |
| **Rhyming and learning to read and spell** | 1 |
| Using the test | 1 |
| Before you start to assess | 1 |
| Diagnostic assessment | 2 |
|     Procedure | 2 |
|     Check for discrimination | 4 |
|     Record sheet | 5 |
|     Scoring | 6 |
| Interpreting the results | 8 |
| **Remediation** | 10 |
| Procedure | 11 |
|     Starting with new words and the complete non-starter | 12 |
| Early training in categorising sounds | 17 |
| **Identifying the causes of reading problems** | 18 |
| Auditory and linguistic factors in learning to read | 19 |
| The cues involved in learning to read and write | 20 |
|     The visual strategy | 20 |
|     The linguistic factor | 20 |
|     Visual and linguistic factors | 22 |
|     Auditory factors | 23 |
|     Auditory discrimination | 24 |
|     Segmentation | 25 |
| **Summary** | 32 |
| **Appendix I    Further research** | 33 |
|     The first project | 33 |
|     The second project | 34 |
|     The training study | 36 |
| **Appendix II    Norms for the sound categorisation test** | 38 |
| **References** | 40 |
| **Further publications** | 44 |

**Summary of test instructions** – For ease of reference this is to be found on the inside back cover.

# Preface

We have always known that it is important to foster the young child's developing language skills. Now we have clear evidence, from research, that word play and rhyming games in the pre-school years have a distinct impact on reading and spelling when the child goes to school.[48]

Over 400 young children were tested on their ability to hear rhyme and alliteration in spoken words (Test 2). None of the children had learned to read. When their reading skills were tested three years later, those who had scored well on the word sound test could read and spell significantly better than those who had scored poorly. Children who scored poorly on this test who were then trained in sound recognition, made remarkable progress in spelling as well as in reading.

It is difficult to discover why a non-reader cannot read using conventional reading tests. This research shows that skill at sound categorisation is important for reading and spelling and can be tested in the non-reader. Test 1, identifies young children and backward readers or non-readers of any age who need special help with sound categorisation. Test 2, can be used with older backward readers. Both tests can be used with children or adults who cannot read or who cannot spell, to identify problems with sound categorisation.

The methods that were used so successfully in the training study were originally developed in successful remedial work with children with severe reading and spelling problems. These methods are outlined in the 'Remediation' section. *Sound Pictures*, the training package, was developed to help pre-readers master sound categorisation skills before they meet words in print.

This revised edition attempts not only to provide new and additional information, but also to make the test more accessible to the practising classroom teacher. Instructions for using the test have been explained and clarified, and there is a new summary of instructions for daily, routine use.

Oxford, January, 1984

# Rhyming and learning to read and spell

## Using the test

This test assesses the ability to recognise rhyme and alliteration in spoken words. Rhyming is a skill acquired very early by young children, and research shows that the child who has this skill when he comes to school makes better progress in reading and spelling. Rhyming is a natural way of categorising words that have sounds in common, and also a natural way to analyse speech units. Both skills are important when we come to use the alphabetic code to learn to read and to spell. It is a major source of difficulty for older children who are backward at reading or spelling. Yet controlled studies show that children who start school with poor sound recognition skills make good progress when they are given specific training.

This test can be used to identify young children who find rhyming difficult and who are likely to encounter problems learning to read and to spell. Identification means that training programmes can be introduced at an early stage before failure occurs. The test is also useful for identifying the problems of older children, so that appropriate remediation can be introduced.

The instructions for the test are very important. Most young children play with and recognise rhymes. The instructions can be modified for older children, but younger children may need more examples in the preliminary word play.

## Before you start to assess

It is commonsense to check the hearing and eyesight of any child who is having difficulty learning to read and write. Even when a child is referred to a medically-orientated centre these checks are not carried out automatically. The parent or the teacher may need to take the initiative to see that such tests are carried out.

Children who have had hearing problems in their pre-school years may have difficulty discriminating between sounds even though their hearing is now said to be perfect. This may be because they did not learn to distinguish between similar sounds in the usual way when they were at the early developmental language stage. They will need to practice these skills now. Results on tests which are dependent on such skills are likely to be unreliable until these skills have been developed.

## Diagnostic assessment

PROCEDURE

Children are seen individually. The assessment should be carried out in a quiet place, where the child will not be distracted by noise and will be able to attend carefully.

The atmosphere should be a relaxed, informal one, where the child is quite at ease. When teacher and child are settled quietly, the teacher can begin by asking the child if he knows a nursery rhyme.

The child may recite a rhyme. If he does, note how well he does this on the test form. But if he does not, and older children may have forgotten them, the teacher may say:

Do you know Hickory dickory dock?
Hickory dickory dock, The mouse ran up the . . . .?
Yes. Clock. Clock/dock. They sound alike, don't they?
Do you know Jack and Jill?
Jack and Jill, Went up the . . . .?
Yes. Hill. Jill/hill. What is another word that sounds like hill?
Teacher: pill    Child . . . .    T. will    C . . . .    T. fill    C . . . .

The child is encouraged to produce words that rhyme, alternately with the teacher. It is a good idea for the teacher to produce rhyming words which are not likely to spring so readily to the child's mind, so that the child is able to produce words which are more familiar and so more readily available to him.

The teacher then introduces a word which is blatantly incorrect. It should be so obvious that the child immediately responds, for example:

T. hat  C. . . . .   T. rat  C. . . . .   T. table  C. . . . .

If there is no quick negative response from the child, the teacher points out the error:

Hat cat rat mat table. That doesn't sound right, does it?

The word games continue until the child realises that he has to indicate when a word is incorrect. This is often realised immediately. Further examples:

T. Can you tell me a word that sounds like bell?
T. bell  C. . . . .   T. well  C. . . . .   T. biscuit  C. . . . .
T. moat  C. . . . .   T. float  C. . . . .   T. toad  C. . . . .
T. mat  C. . . . .   T. fan  C. . . . .
Yes. Biscuit/toad/fan is the odd one out.

The phrase 'doesn't go', or a particular phrase used in class and familiar to the child, may be used instead if this is more appropriate. The same phrase is repeated each time the child spots the incorrect word. The odd word out is made to resemble the other words more closely in each successive trial.

The teacher then says:

Now I am going to say four words, and I want you to tell me which word is the odd one out. Wait until I have said all the words before you tell me which one it is.
Cat hat man fat

If the child is not correct, say so, and give him a second try. If he is still incorrect, say:

Listen again. Cat hat fat man
That's right. Now listen and tell me this time. Man hat fat cat

Explain that the 'odd word out' has simply been said in a different position.

T. Now I want you to say each word after me.
T. cat  C. . . . .   T. hat  C. . . . .   T. man  C. . . . .   T. fat  C. . . . .
Good. Now say these words after me.
T. bell  C. . . . .   T. pet  C. . . . .   T. fell  C. . . . .   T. shell  C. . . . .
Now I will say all of them again, and you can tell me which one is the odd one out. Listen.
Bell pet fell shell
That is very good. Now let us try some others, but I will put the word that sounds different in a different place each time to see if I can catch you out.

## CHECK FOR DISCRIMINATION

A check can be made during these preliminary trials to see if the child is hearing the word correctly, and whether he is articulating correctly. Place a ✓ on the score sheet against words repeated correctly, or record any mispronunciation above the appropriate word. Give further examples if a problem is suspected. Continuing difficulty with discrimination and pronunciation not related to the child's level of development merit separate consideration. More will need to be known about the child's hearing and speech. Remediation may need to be planned in conjunction with a hearing or language therapist if such a referral has been made or seems to be necessary.

The teacher should, as inconspicuously as possible, screen her mouth from the child, using a small card or her hand. This is so that the shape of her mouth does not provide any extra cue for the child. For the same reason each word must be pronounced with equal emphasis, at about two second intervals. If asked, the teacher can repeat the four words but only if the child has not given an answer. No second chance at answering can be accepted. If the child has already given one answer, which is incorrect, his second try will mean that he is only selecting the odd one out of three words, since one will have already been eliminated.

Now proceed through the first list of examples.

Before introducing the second group of words, say:

This next lot is a bit different. Let us have a practice first.

Give the practice examples, and then proceed to the second group of words. After the second group of words, the teacher can say:

That was very good. Let us have a rest for a moment. Can you play *I Spy?* What can you see that begins with . . . . ?

The teacher chooses a sound appropriate to the surroundings, or the first sound of the child's name. The child and teacher alternately suggest appropriate words as in the early examples with the rhyming words. The teacher produces a blatantly inappropriate word again, and waits for the child to spot the error, for example: pin paper pad pencil window.

Three or four turns are given so that the child is not still orientated to the end sounds of the words. He is then advised that it is time to return to the task in hand. He is not told that he is to listen for the word that doesn't start the same as the others.

Give the examples in the final condition.

Altogether the assessment should not take more than ten or fifteen minutes.

RECORD SHEET

With young children it is recommended that the child's name, date of birth, age and the test date be recorded before the assessment session begins. It is important to gain the confidence of a young child, and one who is having difficulty in school may be especially sensitive. The formality of recording such details at the beginning of the session can needlessly and unnecessarily disrupt the developing rapport between the assessor and the child.

It is possible to record the further details on the sheet unobtrusively during the assessment, as follows:

*Nursery rhyme:* if the child repeats a nursery rhyme correctly, mark ✓. If he persistently refuses, mark X. A refusal is very unusual; a child may refuse at first, but will usually join in with one of the rhymes before the preliminaries are completed. What we are looking for is the child who cannot remember a rhyme, or who has the wording muddled, or who exhibits poor articulation. This should be noted on the record sheet, as briefly and as clearly as possible.

*Speech:* record at any time during the session. If the child's speech seems appropriate for his age, mark ✓. If unsure, put a question mark, and pursue at a later date. Sometimes whilst the child repeats the nursery rhyme, or chats, it is possible to detect particular articulation difficulties, for example, confusing c/g or ss/sh; these can be recorded simply, for example, ss/sh. This section can also be completed later from the second part of the record sheet following the repetition of words during the discrimination check.

*Language:* a one word assessment based on the teacher's observation and experience, for example, mature; immature; articulate; monosyllabic: together with ✓ (seems appropriate for age) or X (seems inappropriate for age) can help to round out the developing picture of the child's spoken language.

*Comments:* this space is for any other observation that the teacher feels is appropriate as having a possible bearing on the child's performance. For example, the child may have a heavy cold or catarrh, or be unsettled or not concentrating for some reason. The teacher may be aware of the reason for this, or there may be a perfectly good explanation which is not apparent at the time, such as a family upset or illness. A one word description of the child's behaviour or demeanour can help the teacher in her later assessment of the child's performance, for example: unco-operative; happy; reluctant; over-anxious; craves attention.

SCORING

The scoring for each condition is done in the same way, as illustrated on the sample scored test sheet. If the discrimination check is made during the preliminary trials, place a ✓ beside each word as it is pronounced correctly. If the word is not repeated correctly record the mispronunciation above the appropriate word.

To record the child's reply to the examples in each condition, circle the word he gives as being the 'odd word out' on the record sheet as each example is presented.

At the end of the assessment, total the number of incorrect responses given in each condition. This will give a picture of the child's strengths and weaknessess and should form a reliable basis for the training programme. For example, if the child makes few errors in Conditions 1 and 3, but many errors in Condition 2, he would seem to be able to generalise from one word to another but to need to learn to attend more carefully to words to determine when they share the same mid sound. He may have difficulty analysing words so that initial remediation may need to be based on 'chunks'; see Remediation. If he performs poorly only in Condition 3, he will need to have his attention directed to the words which share the same initial sound.

It should be noted that in the experiments reported earlier, although the backward readers were at a distinct disadvantage in the condition in which three of the four words had the same opening phoneme, the young normal readers also made more errors in this condition than in the rhyming conditions. At present we can only surmise why this should be so. Certainly whilst it is well documented that children use rhyme in word play whilst their language skills are at a very early stage of development, little is said about alliteration.

As words that rhyme usually share a common vowel sound as well as the final consonant it is relatively easy to hear how alike they are, and it is fun to play with them, hence 'jelly-belly'. On the other hand it is quite difficult to think of words that share the same opening consonant and which are followed by a vowel of the same sound and length. Even our alliterative rhymes don't manage it: Peter piper picked a peck of pickled peppers. If they do, they become tongue

# Assessing Reading Difficulties: Test Sheet 1

Name _John Brown_  birth date _17·6·74_  age _5y 6m_  test date _14·1·1980_

nursery rhyme ✓     speech _r/e_

language e.g. _I caught one rabbit which is green_   comments _hay asleep_

## Condition 1

### Last sound different

hat ✓   mat ✓  (fan) ✓  cat ✓
                  _pat_
(doll)   hot  pop   top ✓
      _hop_

sun ✓  gun ✓  (rub)  fun ✓
hen   peg   leg   (beg)
fin   (sit)   pin   win
map   cap   gap   (jam)
cot   hot   fox   (pot)
fill   (pig)   hill   mill
peel   weed   seed   (feed)
pack   lack   sad   (back)

Errors _4_

## Condition 2

### Middle sound different

          _t_
mop ✓  hop  (tap) ✓  lop
pat ✓  (fit) ✓  bat ✓  cat ✓

lot   cot   pot   (hat)
fun   (pin)   bun   gun
hug   dig   (pig)   wig
red   fed   lid   (bed)
wag   rag   bag   (leg)
fell   (doll)   well   bell
dog   fog   jug   (log)
fish   dish   wish   (mash)

Errors _3_

## Condition 3

### First sound different

rot   rod   rock   (box)
lick   lid   (miss)   lip

bud   bun   bus   (rug)
pip   pin   hill   (pig)
ham   tap   had   (hat)
peg   pen   bell   (pet)
fish   fill   fig   (kick)
mop   dog   (doll)   dot
seed   seal   (deep)   seat
room   food   root   (roof)

Errors _5_

## Notes

Child not yet alert to learning. Does not get a lot of chance to talk at home where his two sisters monopolise the conversation.

He is already being left behind in class.

Remediation: Provide opportunity to develop spoken language skills. Give training in categorising sounds, as p.17, with emphasis on John giving the reason for his choices.

twisters: She sells sea shells by the sea shore, but even then the initial consonant has to vary. Certainly these are not 'play' for the very young child, and would seem to be a much later part of language development. It may be that our attention is drawn to the beginnings of words after we see them in print, or when we need to think how a word begins when we are learning to write and spell. Certainly, on the evidence available so far, children seem to categorise words according to sound more easily when the common element is the final sound.

To return to the record sheet, on this assessment children as young as five years of age who are well organised are unlikely to make errors on the first two conditions. Among groups of children of mixed ability however the following error scores can be considered acceptable, See Table 1.

*Table 1*

| Age | 1st Condition | 2nd Condition | 3rd Condition |
|-----|---------------|---------------|---------------|
| 5   | 3             | 3             | 4             |
| 6   | 1             | 1             | 2             |
| 7   | 0             | 0             | 1             |
| 8   | 0             | 0             | 0             |

**Interpreting the results**

If the child's error scores are outside the acceptable limits we should first consider the results in the light of the information recorded at the top of the assessment sheet. If this indicates that the child was content in the test situation, and that the speech and language development seemed unremarkable, remediation will concentrate on the concept of learning to generalise from one word to another. It is possible that, although the child's speech and language seemed unremarkable, the comment section indicated that he was over-anxious. Since he clearly found the task difficult, this is not surprising. However, if the comment section indicates that the child was not concentrating or was distressed for some reason which did not seem to be connected with the task, the teacher must consider whether this had a bearing on the results.

If the child has not been able to repeat a nursery rhyme, and/or his language is confined to one word answers to questions, very restricted or muddled and disorganised, the teacher will need to consider why this should be so. She should not be surprised at the child's failure to make progress since experience of spoken language is essential if the child is to learn to categorise sounds. His poor performance might be because of impoverished language skills or because he has lacked the opportunity to develop adequate language skills; he may be disturbed or withdrawn; he may have a poor auditory memory; or he may have a hearing loss.

The teacher's observation and her knowledge of the child and his situation will help her decide what action to take. Remediation and resources may well be available within the classroom. However the teacher may feel that other expertise, for example, a language therapist, educational psychologist or remedial adviser; is needed to offer practical help or advice. Certainly the child will need to have a programme which considers his special needs in conjunction with the remediation suggested, since he must be helped to develop his language skills. Without digressing too far into this area, I would like to make a plea for a return to singing games, rhymes and jingles, especially for children who need help to organise their spoken language and with auditory memory training. Singing games have both a tune and movements to help us remember the words. Furthermore, each word inevitably has one beat of the tune for each syllable, so polysyllabic words are more likely to be pronounced in the right order. How else would we all have learned to sing 'Su per cal i frag il is tic ex pi al id oc ious'?

A child who is seen to have a definite speech problem will benefit from the advice available from the speech therapist and it is wise to see that the child's hearing has been checked.

# Remediation

Let us first consider remediation for children who are not making the progress in reading and spelling that is expected of them but let us presume that they do know that print stands for the spoken word. They are aware that they can use their language experience and their predictive skills as well as the context of a passage to help them to read.

These children may recognise only a few words or may have developed quite a reasonable sight vocabulary. Some of these children will have great difficulty analysing words, or in synthesising sounds to make new words. Others may have a problem differentiating between letters that look alike; or in naming letters or sounds.

One particular problem for children when they try to categorise words that sound alike is the abstract and transitory nature of speech. Although they can repeat the words there is nothing tangible or concrete for them to compare or manipulate. Even when the student lists words that go together in some way he may not recognise the common element that links them.

It is rather like the child's problem with numbers. He may be able to give you five cubes, but not be able to tell you the answer to 3 + 2 or 4 + 1. So we would show him how to arrange the cubes on the table so that he can see that 3 and 2 are integral parts of 5.

In reading, one way of coping with these problems with words is to use the Alpha-beta plastic script letters, available from most toy shops. These letters feel different from each other – a, e, i, o, u, are tactually quite dissimilar. They are not reversible and are colour coded. Children who have difficulty remembering sound/symbol associations, or differentiating between letters that look alike, learn these associations and discriminations quite quickly when they use these tangible letters. The letters can be arranged until the word is correct before it is written down, eliminating both the humiliation of failure, and the establishment of incorrect motor patterns.

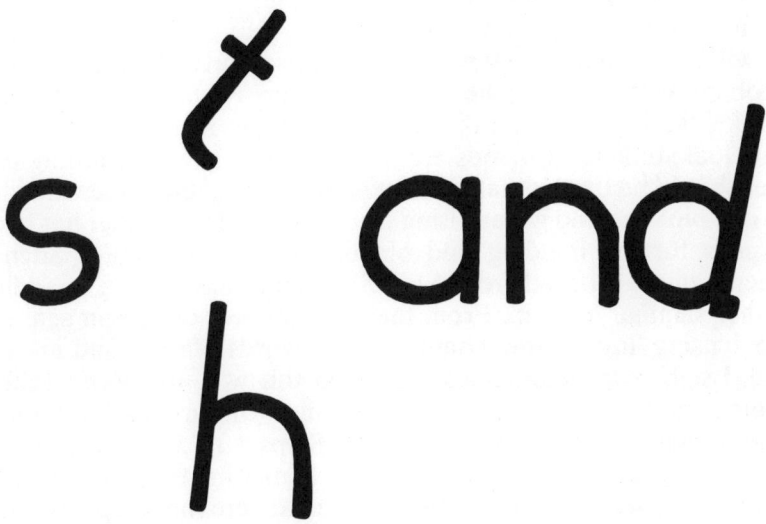

**Procedure**

Have the box of letters on the table.
1  Ask the child to use the letters to make a word that he already knows, for example, and.
2  Now ask him to say a word that sounds like 'and', for example: land, sand, hand or band.
3  Ask him to change 'and' into the new word, for example, sand. Then ask him to change it into another word that he has given you.

It is surprising how difficult this is for some children. The important point we must make is that the letters a.n.d. stay on the table and do not change even though the word keeps changing. We must continue to point out that the words share this common element 'and'. Most children will not be ready to go beyond 'and sand hand land stand', if they have a real problem.

The more able student can continue to add and subtract letters to make new words, for example: and sand stand standing understand; and hand handsome; and grand grandma grandpa; and candle handle. Use only words proposed by the student.

4    The words that have been made with the letters are recorded in a word group book kept for the purpose. Head the list of words 'and'. Use cursive script.

5    The words are used in written work.

It will be noted that, in this instance, the student will not experience a problem with blending the sounds together. We have started with a 'chunk', 'and'. Progress takes place according to the needs of the individual student. If blends are a problem, only words adding one letter should be used initially, for example: sand, land. Once the idea of word building and generalising from one word to another has been grasped, further building and blends can be introduced. Such a student might proceed from Step 5 to: and land landing – adding another familiar 'chunk'. From there the student can begin again at Step 1 using 'ing' as the 'chunk'. Other words often found in very limited sight vocabularies and useful in this way are: went, (alter, keeping the 'ent'); in; and it. By the time word groups using these 'chunks' have been established, as in Steps 1 to 5, the use of the individual letters to establish the initial 'chunks' has frequently helped the pupil to begin to learn how the 'chunks' are made up. In other words he is also learning that the single speech unit is made up of more than one letter when it is written down, and he has begun to learn how to build these units.

STARTING WITH NEW WORDS AND THE COMPLETE NON-STARTER

Now it is time for the student to tackle new words that he needs. It is always important for the words to come from the student's own vocabulary and interests. If he has a problem retrieving words from memory, he is much more likely to be able to produce a word which he uses and which is related to things which interest him. He will find it difficult to analyse a word suggested by the teacher if his first problem is remembering what the word is![14]

Let him suggest the new word. Ask him to say it, and then to try to identify the first sound of the word: for example, 'crash'/'c'. Let him select the correct plastic letter, or show him which it is. Let him say the word again, stopping after the next sound if he can: 'crash/cr', and let him select the next letter. Then, 'crash/cra'. Select the next letter. Then, 'crash/sh'. Introduce the fact that s.h. together usually represent the sound 'sh'.

The student who has difficulty analysing words will find this very hard, but unless he can start with a 'chunk' that he knows, it is still better to begin with the word he wants to learn. After the first few times it does become easier. One spur to success is the impermanence of the 'plastic letter' word. It can so easily be altered. He may be wrong, but this can be changed so easily leaving no trace of the incorrect version to indicate the failure.

Once the word has been made correctly, the letters are jumbled up, and the student tries to make the word again. When he can make the word successfully without help, other points are introduced systematically.[7] The first point for our purpose here is to choose a basis for categorising this word with others. It can be grouped with other 'cr' words, or 'ash' words, or 'sh' words. It is best to choose the category most suited to the student's current vocabulary and other useful words he may need; perhaps related to the subject he is writing about. The words are again suggested by the student, and made using the plastic letters; with the relevant letters, for example, 'sh', staying on the table, as in Steps 1 to 5. The word group will be recorded under the appropriate heading.

The plastic letters are ideal for word building. The vowels are all one colour so it is easy to see whether each syllable contains at least one vowel. Rules are introduced as they arise. As Cotterell points out, no regular word needs learning, as it can be worked out.[46] If the child can write 'hip' he can write hippopotamus. It often helps to make this point with the student who feels competent to write only one syllable words. A simplified version of this approach to regular words is as follows.

Regular words, for example,    re mem ber    up set

1  Say the word clearly and correctly.
2  Say the word in syllables, tap it out if necessary.
3  Rule: each syllable must contain at least one vowel.
4  Make the word with the plastic letters, vocalising as he does so. Write the word, vocalising as he writes.
5  Relate the word to other words that can be categorised with it.

But what about words that cannot be 'sounded out'. It is often said that all words can be grouped in some way, and that no words are really irregular. Nevertheless many children do have a problem remembering 'chunks', such as 'igh' in 'high' and 'light', and sequences such as 'ought'. How are they to learn to recognise them? As we have said many times, for so many children who are unable to categorise sounds each word appears unique.

Once again the plastic letters prove invaluable for introducing these sequences. Often the student *knows* more than he realises. He may say that he cannot tell you how to write 'out', but he can repeat the old rhyme 'o.u.t. spells out and out you must go'.

Irregular sequences can be introduced using the plastic letters, and the student can again categorise the words by their sounds and learn to group them accordingly, again following Steps 1 to 5. But if he does not know the letters he needs for the word the teacher can tell him which ones he needs. After the word has been made, it is jumbled up again, and the student makes it once more. For example, change 'light' to 'fight fright right sight sigh high.' Again the student must realise that 'igh' letters stay on the table all the time, whilst the words change around them.

It is again particularly important for the student to suggest the words. The words will be recorded, using cursive script, as before. If the words are not ones in the student's current vocabulary he may attach the wrong label to a word. Students sometimes develop correct writing patterns for words which they then fail to label correctly because the word has not been meaningful for them.

Irregular words can be learned using the multi-sensory technique where each letter is named, not sounded, as it is written. Once the correct motor pattern has been established the naming of the letters can be discontinued. This form of Simultaneous Oral Spelling was first described by Gillingham and Stillman.[47]

This author has used this technique successfully with adults and children who have been unable to read or to spell, and who have not been able to distinguish between the different letters. This has been done as described, taking any word, no matter how difficult, provided the student wants to learn it, making it first with the plastic letters, and then recording it in the following manner.

Irregular words, for example, light, ought.
1   Have the word written correctly, or made with the letters.
2   Say the word.

3   Write the word, spelling out each letter as it is written, using cursive script. So as the student sees each letter, he hears its name and also receives kinaesthetic feedback through the movement of the arm and throat muscles. This not only reinforces sound/symbol association but also sequencing and recall in each modality, whilst the correct motor pattern is established.
4   Check to see if the word is correct. Cover it up and repeat the process.

The student is required to practice the word three times a day, which takes approximately thirty seconds, for five or six consecutive days. This is a most effective way of learning to read and write words when all else has failed. It must not deteriorate into rote spelling, which is an entirely different thing. Of course the word learned is related to others in the same sound family. He must make this generalisation from one word to another to reduce his learning load.

In recent experiments conducted by the author this adaptation of this method has proved to be more effective than other methods which omitted either the writing or the naming. In other words children who were severely retarded in reading and spelling had far more success using this method to learn to read and write new words, and remembered them more successfully when retested a month later. The importance of establishing motor patterns for spelling, and as a way to learn to read, has long been recognised. However it is the successful organisation of the correct motor patterns that is important and especially for backward readers and spellers who have particular difficulty in remembering the patterns so that they can reproduce them consistently. This unorthodox approach does prove effective and can be used as a starting point; once one word has been learned the student can begin to learn to generalise from that word to another one.

More than once in this section I have stressed the use of cursive writing and the need to develop correct motor patterns for words. The importance of the latter has been amply demonstrated in these recent experiments. But how many people recognise the importance of cursive writing to the development of reading skill?

The copying experiment emphasised the importance of seeing the word as a meaningful unit. Those children who used cursive script when they copied the text made fewer errors than the children who used print. Furthermore, their work was easier to read. When letters are joined together in words in a plain cursive script, the words are seen as visual units, since the spaces fall automatically *between* the words. Children who are poor readers often have difficulty organising their visuo spatial skills. Look back at the previous line of print and imagine having difficulty deciding which letters belong together! It will be much easier for the child to read his own work if he uses 'joined up' writing so that he sees *words,* not letters and spaces.

Handwriting must be taught. The child must learn to start and finish each letter in the correct place, so that he will automatically write from left to right and join the letters naturally to one another. Using the plastic letters to make the word first provides an excellent opportunity for handwriting to be introduced correctly. As the child does not write the word down until it is correct he is prevented from forming bad habits and incorrect writing of both the letters and words.

The complete non-starter will begin by suggesting sentences for his own book, and these will be made using the plastic letters as indicated. After the words and then sentences have been made, and re-made, with the letters they will be recorded, perhaps illustrated by the student, then typed by the teacher. The same words are also used to type new stories so that they are recognised in different contexts. The word categories are taken from the words produced by the child and recorded in a separate book as already discussed. This combination, using the child's own language and the tactile medium of the plastic letters to help him to learn to organise and categorise sounds, has proved unfailingly successful with many children and adults.

**Early training in categorising sounds**

Since it has been shown that the ability to categorise sounds seems to be important for learning to read and to spell, and that many four-year old children are able to do this quite happily, we can try to help those young children who are not categorising sounds successfully before they begin to read and to spell.
There are several ways that we can do this.

1. Let the child identify objects or pictures which share a given sound. For example:
    a) Find me pictures of things that start with 'b'.
    b) Find me pictures of things that start with the same as this one – show a picture of a bus.
    c) What sound do all the things in these pictures start with? Have sound common to group.
    d) Which picture doesn't begin with 'b'?
    e) Which picture doesn't start with the same sound as the others?
    f) Which pictures go together? All but one have the chosen sound in common.
    g) Child gives the *reason* for his choice.

2. The ability to explain why words do or do not go together gives a true idea of whether or not the child has grasped the real concept for categorising the words.

3. Stages a) to g) can be repeated without the use of pictures, and for the mid and first sound of the words as well as the final sound.

# Identifying the causes of reading problems

Many children have difficulty learning to read and to spell. Although tests are available to help the teacher assess the progress the child has made, these tests are primarily designed for children who can already read and generally do not give any information about the causes of the child's problem. This manual, on the other hand, has been written to help teachers assess skills related to learning to read in children who have made little or no progress or whose failure to progress beyond the most basic level is puzzling.

No one simple assessment could claim to provide the whole answer to such children's problems as so many factors are involved. Even the definition of what reading is will vary from one discipline to another.[1] Certainly reading is a complex learned skill. Learning to read requires a great deal of the child: his capacity to learn; motivation and concentration; and the ability to direct attention. The reader must be able to understand language, and also be able to analyse it at a sophisticated level. Visual and auditory perception are involved as are learning, memory and rule formation. So it is unlikely that children having problems with the acquisition of written language all experience the same difficulties. Indeed, given the individual characteristics of the children themselves and the complex nature of the reading process, it would be surprising if they did. There has of course been a good deal of research aimed at identifying distinct forms of reading problems.[2,3,4] Unfortunately such research has so far produced little in the way of general conclusions. Often the observational skills of the teacher will be the most important factor in determining the reasons for the child's failure to make progress.[5]

A solution for childrens' reading problems has been sought in many different areas, and different disciplines have looked at the problem according to their own academic specialities. Many studies in psychology, medicine, education and neurology have confirmed that backward readers frequently have different problems one from another, but have not proved very helpful in establishing the precise nature of these problems. Three possible reasons for this can be examined. Firstly, the number of backward readers considered in these studies has often been too small for groups who have similar problems to be identified.[6] Secondly, the backward readers have frequently been asked to perform tasks which seem to have only the most tenuous links with reading and writing, in that they do not involve words at all. And finally, studies comparing backward with normal readers have traditionally compared children of the same age and intellectual level, the only difference between the groups being in how far they have learned to read.[2] The trouble with this design is that any difference which is found between the groups might just as well be the result of the backward readers' limited experience in reading as a cause of their reading problem. These three problems are not inseparable. There seems to be a need for studies designed to compare large groups of backward and normal readers of normal intelligence who are reading at the same level. This ensures that any differences found are not merely a consequence of the poor readers' limited reading experience. Very large groups increase the chances of finding clinical sub-groups. These groups need to be compared on tasks involving words, if they are to prove more helpful in answering our questions about reading failure.[7]

**Auditory and linguistic factors in learning to read**

Working with children, and adults, who have difficulty with both reading and spelling has taught me that though their backgrounds, experience, and indeed overall problems often seem very different one from another, they frequently share a common inability to generalise from one word to another. They seem to regard each word they learn as unique. They do not seem able to apply what they learn about words they can read to new words when they occur. This means that reading remains a laborious word by word decoding task.

Reading the sentence 'Stay and play with me to-day', the child may struggle to decode the word 'stay', but then fail to use this information to help him to read 'play' and 'to-day'. The poor speller may show this same inability to generalise from one word to another. He may know quite well how to write 'and', yet fail to see how this can help him to write 'sand', 'stand', or 'landing'.

## The cues involved in learning to read and to write

### THE VISUAL STRATEGY

Why is it that some children cannot generalise from one word to another? As reading is a visual task, is it because they cannot see that 'sand' and 'hand' have similar visual patterns? Most children in this country are initially taught to read by the whole word method, which is wholly dependent on the visual recognition of patterns.[8] Signs and labels are printed for classroom pictures and objects and the child is required to learn the printed label. In fact from a very early stage children seem able to recognise quite complex visual patterns such as 'aeroplane'.

It is certainly more efficient to read visual 'chunks', that is words or phrases, than to read letter by letter. At the level of the individual letter English Orthography is highly variable, since particular letters often signify different sounds in different words.[9] This variability is likely to get smaller the larger the chunk of letters which the child takes in.[10,11] Thus the letter 'o' will pose a problem when considered as an individual unit in 'pod', 'wrote', 'soak', 'foot' and 'pool', but if considered as part of the stable sequence 'ought' is non-variable. Obviously it will help a child to recognise such sequences as wholes, rather than having to build them up letter by letter or phoneme by phoneme. A recent Japanese study has shown that very young children are able to learn to recognise very complex visual patterns provided they are meaningful.[12] So is it enough just to be able to match words on their visual appearance when we see them in print?

### THE LINGUISTIC FACTOR

There is evidence that young children learning to read adopt a visual strategy which takes them straight to the meaning of the word.[13]

Children whose ages ranged from 6½ to 13½ years were given picture-word pairs and asked to say whether the items rhymed, in a sound task, or 'went together' in a meaning task. The children had to say 'double, double, double' out aloud whilst doing the task. This affected the time taken for the sound task, where the children had to attend to the sound patterns of the words, but not the meaning task. Even the youngest children were successful on this latter task despite the interference. Barron & Baron concluded that children can get meaning from printed words without the use of an intermediate phonemic code.

Will matching patterns visually help reading then, if the name of the pattern is not known? Will matching the patterns of words that they cannot read help backward readers? Probably not, since without a label the written word remains a pattern, and not a word at all. It is necessary to know the meaning of the pattern. Even if the child can see that 'hand' has a visual pattern like 'sand' this will not help him unless he knows that the letters s.a.n.d. together make the word 'sand'. He must first be able to attach a label to the visual pattern. He must learn that print is the visual representation of the language that he sees and hears.

What happens if the child does not know what the pattern is called? The connection between different verbal difficulties has been demonstrated in a detailed case study of a backward reader where the major problem appeared to be a word finding difficulty.[14] This study reports the case of a backward reader who had no difficulty reproducing complex visual patterns, for example: laugh, saucer, high. But as he could not remember the names of these patterns, he could not use his ability to help him name other similar words. Nor could he name the letters, so he was unable to use an alternative strategy to learn to read. Jansky and de Hirsch have demonstrated that one of the best ways of predicting how quickly a child will learn to read is to look at how well he can name the letters of the alphabet when he arrives at school.[15] Work by Audley suggests that poor readers are slower at naming, and that they have difficulty in dealing with the speech aspect of the names.[6]

The able reader uses his linguistic skill as well as the context of the passage to predict and determine his choice of words when he reads, and does not examine the visual detail of each written word minutely.[16] His experience with language reinforces his interpretation of the printed word. Nevertheless he must be able to remember common patterns, and to detect differences between them. This will be particularly important when he is reading new words in a new context.

VISUAL AND LINGUISTIC FACTORS

We have all met the child who recognises 'sometimes', but cannot read 'some' or 'times'. There are occasions when the context or our linguistic skill is not enough to help us determine the pronunciation of a word precisely. Then we must pay more attention to the detail within words. Some recent experiments have shown that poor readers fail to do this efficiently. In two studies backward and normal readers, both normal in intelligence, were compared on tasks related to reading and spelling. Both groups were reading at about the seven year level, so the normal readers were about seven-years old though the average age of the backward readers was about ten years. In the first task, the children were shown a series of four letter words, one at a time. Each child looked at the word for five seconds, and then had to reproduce it immediately using Letraset letters printed on small cards. Although the backward readers were not quite as efficient at this task both groups were more or less equivalent in their ability to reproduce the words. However the backward readers who made errors made more errors at the ends of words, and inverted and reversed more letters.[17]

In the second study three groups of children were asked to copy printed prose passages. These were the large group of ten-year old backward readers, a second group of ten-year old children not backward in reading, and the younger group of children reading normally for their age and intelligence and at the same reading level as the backward readers. The backward readers were much slower and made many more errors than the normal readers of the same age on this copying task.[18] The older able readers copied the text in meaningful units of words or phrases. But the backward readers and the young normal readers copied at the level of the individual letter not using meaningful units to improve their performance. It is not surprising that they were slow and inaccurate, as their strategy forced them to make frequent visual checks. But the normal readers seem to organise their visual perceptual skills in some way as they grow older and more skilled in reading. The crucial variable seems to be the reference unit used, the word as a meaningful unit. These studies suggest that the visual detail and the linguistic content of printed words are both important for reading. In fact several studies have shown that training in visual discrimination between shapes by itself does not improve word *recognition*. [19] [20] [21] A recent study by this author has also shown that both backward and normal readers can equally well detect visual similarities and differences in written words when they are not required to read them.

The ability to generalise from one word to another when reading cannot therefore be dependent on matching visual patterns alone. This was indeed shown to be the case when the same backward and normal readers were required to distinguish similarities and differences between words when the words were presented aurally. A striking difference was found when the words were spoken, the backward readers being at a distinct disadvantage in this situation.[22]

AUDITORY FACTORS

This should perhaps not surprise us, as reading and writing involve translating spoken language into a visual representation. So hearing will be important to normal reading skill development and this has been widely demonstrated with studies with deaf children. [23] [24] [25] [26] Although interpretation is complicated by the fact that these children have impoverished language skills, those deaf children who do learn to read seem to reach a plateau in their reading and the difference between their progress and that of hearing children appears to be progressively greater as they get older. [24] [10] [27] Conrad shows that even in the case of deaf children, who more than anyone might find ways of depending on vision in reading, those who were aware of similarities in sounds (rhymes) learned to read much better than the rest.

In general then it is agreed that learning to read follows on from and utilises the child's already well developed oral language abilities. Although the child may make early progress in reading through 'whole word' instruction, there eventually comes a point at which phonics must be introduced for further progress to be made.[28] [10] If he cannot recognise the visual pattern that he sees, and the context of the passage does not allow him to guess what the word is, he must have some other way of working it out. If he is to use a phonetic strategy the child will need to know the names of the letters, to be able to generalise from one word to another, to differentiate one sound from another and to segment speech, so it is clear that the accurate perception of speech will be important. Many investigators considering the relation of auditory perception to reading have simply examined speech sound discrimination.

AUDITORY DISCRIMINATION

The usual finding in studies investigating the relationship between speech sound discrimination and reading ability is that poor reading ability is associated with poor auditory discrimination. Such studies usually employ the Wepman test of Auditory Discrimination, which comes in two parallel forms each consisting of forty pairs of single syllable words. Thirty pairs differ by one phoneme while ten pairs are identical and the child is required to make a same/different judgement as each pair is read to him by the examiner. One unfortunate consequence of this imbalance is that response bias leads to an increase in the number of 'same' responses, so the test is liable to underestimate the subject's discriminative ability.[29] Nevertheless the test does relate to reading ability. Clark found that poor readers performed poorly on tests of auditory discrimination, but made the important point that her study could not establish whether poor auditory discrimination was a cause of their failure in reading, or whether success in reading might have helped the development of such discrimination.[30] In other words, learning to read might help children to organise their auditory perception. Wepman himself says that sounds will be interpreted in relation to previous experience.[31]

This criticism does not however apply to the longitudinal study of de Hirsch et al who found that performance on the Wepman test in kindergarten was one of the best predictors of subsequent reading difficulties when children were tested two years later.[32]

A further question is the source of this relationship between speech sound discrimination and reading ability. The paired comparison procedure used in this test clearly involves complex processes: each pair of items must be attended to, retained, compared and a vocal same/different response made. Thus we cannot conclude that poor test performance necessarily reflects poor speech perception.

The only attempt to examine in more detail the factors involved in performing the Wepman test was made by Blank.[33] Although the first part of this study replicated the relationship found between poor reading and poor auditory discrimination, overall the results suggested that other factors apart from the perception of speech sounds influence performance on the Wepman test.

However auditory perception involves much more than the basic discrimination of speech sounds. In explaining reading problems we must take account of the fact that backward readers are usually able to hear the words they are asked to read and spell, and can usually repeat them.

SEGMENTATION

Another aspect of auditory perception which seems important for learning to read involves the segmentation of speech. Savin suggests that although backward readers can segment speech into syllables they do not comprehend that for two syllables to rhyme they must be identical except for one segment. They do not understand that syllables can be analysed into shorter segments.[34]

Liberman and her colleagues have investigated the relationship between the ability to segment speech into phonemes (sounds) and reading ability.[35] In this study, four-, five-, and six-year old children had to learn to tap out the number (from one to three) of segments in a list of test words which were read to them. Deciding how many syllables were in a word was much easier at all ages than deciding the number of phonemes in a word. A follow-up study showed that children who could tell the number of phonemes in a word were making more progress in reading, although in a further paper the authors suggest that this implied connection could in fact have resulted from reading instruction or intellectual maturation.[36] They suggest too, however, that a deficiency in speech segmentation ability may be the reason that poor readers make many errors on consonants at the end of words when they read.[37]

In fact one of the most difficult concepts for the child learning to read and to spell is that units of speech, the syllable and the word, are represented by smaller units in the alphabetic script. But if we are to read and spell we must use the alphabet, and the alphabetic code works by breaking words down into constituent sounds, that is, units smaller than the syllable. The child learning to read and spell must come to understand that one unit of speech can be represented by more than one unit in the alphabetic script.

So although 'butterfly' has three speech units, or syllables, they are represented by nine letters in the printed word. 'Bag' though only one speech unit, is represented by three letters. The child would not read 'butterfly' instead of 'bag' if he were looking for a word with three phonemic (sound) segments to correspond to the printed word 'bag', instead of looking for a word with three speech (syllabic) units.

This complex and abstract relationship between alphabetic writing and speech seems to be a major problem in early reading acquisition.[38] The child does not need to understand this relationship when he is talking. In spoken language words are probably perceived in units which are at least a syllable in length, and certainly not as conglomerations of phonemes.[39,40]

It is easy to see that recognising the similarities in sound between different spoken words is likely to be important in learning to read. If we do not recognise these similarities each word we learn to read will appear unique. Children learn to group words according to sound quite spontaneously in word play as they grow up.[41] One only has to listen to three-year olds at the tea-table, saying: jelly-belly, honey-bunny. Bullock suggests that the best way to develop children's ability to discriminate and recognise the relationships between letters and sounds could be by a return to the use of rhymes, jingles and alliteration in the classroom,[42] categorising words according to their sounds.

The ability to recognise that syllables sound alike, but are still dissimilar as wholes, that is to say rhyming words, or words with the same first sounds, would seem to indicate tacit acknowledgement of the fact that the spoken syllable unit can be represented by more than one graphemic (written) unit. That is, if 'cat' and 'hat' rhyme, but are different words, they must be made up of more than one unit. We can see why auditory discrimination is not enough. Clearly auditory analysis is also necessary. Does this mean that if the child appreciates rhyme he can break syllables up into their constituent parts?

Unfortunately this does not necessarily follow. When a child does realise that 'cat' and 'mat' have a sound in common he has broken down each monosyllabic word into smaller units and has categorised the two words as similar because they have one of these units in common, that is, 'at'. But this knowledge may not be explicit. The child may recognise rhymes without an explicit appreciation that the words share a common element. Simply to produce a word that rhymes is not enough.[43] The fact that the child produces a word which 'sounds the same', as young children clearly do in word play, for example 'mat' and 'hat', does not mean that he appreciates or makes this generalisation. Any teacher of backward readers will be familiar with this situation. The child wishes to write a word that he does not know, for example, 'way'. Asked to think of a word that he does know that sounds similar, he says 'day'. But he still cannot appreciate how this can help him.

This insensitivity means that each word he learns is unique. The remedial implications are overwhelming. Failure to recognise such a difficulty would render remediation ineffective. The child must be able to group together words which are different but which have sounds in common if he is to learn the rules of reading and writing. He must understand that 'way', 'day', and 'pay' though different, nevertheless have a sound in common. That this difficulty might be an important factor in reading and spelling failure has been demonstrated recently.[44]

Three groups of children took part in this study, and these were the same groups of children who were described as taking part in the experiments detailed on page 22. All the children attended normal schools, but many of the 62 backward readers were receiving remedial help. The average age of this group was over ten-years old, but their average reading age, as measured by the Neale analysis of reading ability, was only 7½ years. Their average spelling age was even lower. The details of this group are presented in Table 2.

*Table 2*
Details of the two groups

|  | N | Age Mean | Age Range | IQ (WISC) Mean | IQ (WISC) Range | Reading age (Neale) Mean | Reading age (Neale) Range | Spelling age (Schonell) Mean | Spelling age (Schonell) Range |
|---|---|---|---|---|---|---|---|---|---|
| Backward readers | 60 | 10yr 4mth | 8yr 4mth – 13yr 5mth | 108.7 | 93–137 | 7yr 7mth | 6yr – 9yr 4mth | 6yr 10mth | 5yr – 8yr 9mth |
| Normal readers | 30 | 6yr 10mth | 5yr 8mth – 8yr 7mth | 107.9 | 93–119 | 7yr 6mth | 6yr – 9yr 2mth | 7yr 2mth | 5yr 1mth – 10yr 2mth |

The group of young normal readers were reading at the same level as the backward readers. Now although these two groups were reading at the same level and were both of normal intelligence for their age, the backward readers were on average over three years older than the younger group. However if, in the design, the backward readers are worse at recognising when words share a common element, the fact that the two groups have reached the same reading level as one another rules out the possibility that the backward readers perceptual failure is merely the result of a lack of reading experience. As the two groups are reading at the same level such a failure could suggest that the backward readers may have a major difficulty in the organisation of auditory perception.

The third group of children were the same age as the backward readers, but reading normally for their age. This is the traditional comparison in studies of reading backwardness.

Three tasks were presented to the groups. In the first task the children were required to detect which one of four spoken words did not share the sound common to the other three words. In the second task the children were required to produce a word to rhyme with a word spoken by the examiner. In the third task the children were required to detect which one of four written words did not share the letter common to the other three written words.

In practice trials to ensure that the children understood the first task, two of the children in the large group of backward readers and spellers failed on several occasions to recall the four words which they had been asked to repeat. In order that subsequent failure on the spoken tasks could not be attributed to a memory failure these two children were not included in the aural experiment. The group of backward readers and spellers therefore number 60 in this first task. However it must be pointed out that nearly all the children in the group of young normal readers failed to recall the words in the practice trials.

The children in each group were seen individually. The experimenter talked to the child about nursery rhymes, and about words that sound similar to each other. Word play was encouraged, and practice trials ensured that each child understood and could perform the oddity task before testing began.

The method which was used to test the grouping of sounds was to say four monosyllabic words to the child. Three of the words had a sound in common which the fourth did not share. The child had to say which was the odd word out. There were three series, each with six trials, 18 trials in all. In the first series, all four words always had the same middle phoneme but the last two phonemes were the same in three words while the odd word had a different final phoneme, for example: weed peel need deed. Another series was the same except that the middle phoneme was different in the odd word. Thus the experimenter would say: red fed nod bed, and the child would have to say that the odd word out was 'nod'. In the third series of trials three words had the same opening phoneme while the odd one did not, for example: hat pen pig pup. The position of the odd word varied systematically in all three series.

Great care was taken to pronounce each word with the same emphasis so that the child was not given any additional cue to the correct word. The experimenter also always hid her mouth from the child's view with a card, so that the shape of her mouth would not provide any additonal cue for any of the children.

The results were simply scored on the number of errors each child made out of the six trials in each of the three series. This experiment produced a startling difference between the group of backward readers and the young normal readers. The backward readers made more errors than the younger children in all three series, and were at a particular disadvantage with the series in which three of the four words had the same opening phoneme. Putting the series together, 91.66% of the 60 backward readers made errors and 85% made more than one error. Only 53.3% of the young normal readers made errors and only 26.66% more than one. This difference is all the more remarkable given that the backward reading group was actually of a considerably higher intellectual level than the younger normal reading group as they were older by an average of 3½ years. Surprisingly the young children could say which was the odd word out even though they were often unable to recall the four words.

A further finding was that a clear developmental trend was evident among these younger normal readers. Those few children in this group who made more than one error were younger and had lower intelligence scores and reading and spelling ages than the rest of their group. All these differences were significant. The group of older normal readers made no errors at all. This suggests that as they grow older the normal readers become more proficient at organising and categorising sounds and get better at reading and spelling.

It can also be suggested that many backward readers may be held back by a particular difficulty with organising sounds. No developmental trend was found among the backward readers; here the only significant difference was that the few children who made one or no errors had a significantly higher spelling age than the rest. So difficulty in organising sounds may have particularly harmful effects on spelling among backward readers.

The second task efficiently demonstrated that inadvertent stress had not been responsible in any way for the results in the first experiment, and confirmed the backward readers' difficulty at categorising sounds. The children were asked to produce a word which rhymed with each of ten spoken words. Here no extraneous cues of emphasis could possibly provide the correct answer. Again, despite their superior age and overall intellectual ability, the backward readers were far worse than the normal readers on this task. Of the backward reading group 38.33% failed to produce a rhyming word in one or more trials, compared with only 6.66% of the younger normal readers. Although a different type of task to the oddity test, the relative failure of the backward readers is striking confirmation of their difficulty with categorising sounds.

The third task, the visual condition, has already been mentioned. The three groups of children were asked to select the odd one out of four words which were presented written on a card. As in the aural study, three of the words had a letter in common which the fourth did not share. Again there were six trials in each of three series. As the children were not asked to read the words their selection of the odd word out could depend entirely on their detection of visual similarities and differences in the written words.

The results in this visual condition were in marked contrast to those in the auditory experiments. Although the backward readers were worse than the young normal readers reading at the same level, 86.6% of the former and 92.26% of the latter made no errors at all, and this difference between the groups in this visual condition was not significant. The older normal readers again made no errors. This result strongly suggests that the majority of children in both groups have no problem detecting visual similarities and differences in written words.

Further confirmation that the ability to categorise sounds is particularly important for reading and spelling was obtained in the study reported on page 22. The groups of backward and normal readers were asked to reproduce the words they had been shown using the Letraset letters. As already stated there was no significant difference between the groups in their ability to reproduce the words in this visual condition. But in the cross-modal conditions in this experiment, where the children were asked to read the words, or to make given words, that is, spell, the backward readers were much less successful than the normal readers. There was a very significant difference between the groups in their ability to read and to spell the words. This was very puzzling since the groups had been carefully matched on their reading levels. A closer look revealed a probable reason for this discrepancy in the reading and spelling conditions in this particular study. The young normal readers who did badly in the visual condition had in fact succeeded on the sound categorising task in the other experiment. Consequently when they were asked to read or to spell these new words, they were able to use a phonetic strategy. The backward readers who were unsuccessful at reproducing the words in this visual task, however, had also failed on the sound categorisation tasks. So they had no alternative phonetic strategy for reading and spelling the words.

An earlier study with these same children had demonstrated the importance of phonological cues for spelling.[45] In this study the children were simply asked to read 18 words on one occasion and then to write the same words on another occasion. The two skills of reading and spelling were surprisingly separate in both groups in that children could read words which they could not spell and spell words which they could not read. This discrepancy was greater in the backward readers. Further analysis suggested that at this early stage of reading and spelling both groups used phonological cues in spelling more than in reading. This is not surprising, for until they can remember the patterns for all the words they wish to write they must develop a strategy for coding them which uses the alphabet.

Taken together these experiments provide overwhelming evidence that the ability to categorise sounds is important in both reading and spelling, and that this seems to be a major source of difficulty for backward readers. Undoubtedly one of the underlying factors for success in both reading and spelling will be the development of this ability to organise and categorise sounds. Recognition of this factor has important implications for teaching.

# Summary

Although vision is our primary and obvious medium for reading, we must not forget that we are scanning the written representation of spoken language. So that each word does not appear to be unique we must learn to generalise from one written word to another. To do this we must consider the linguistic content of the visual pattern, its aural and spoken counterpart.

The categorisation of sounds is an important factor in the development of reading skill, and of particular importance to backward readers in learning to spell. Normal children seem to develop these skills as their reading progresses but backward readers do not.

One way to tell whether a student can determine when words share a common element is to see if he can categorise them according to sound. The student's ability to categorise words in this way can be assessed by asking him to determine the odd word out of four spoken words, three of which share a common element, as in the examples in this manual.

Suggestions are made which may be relevant for remedial teaching.

Lynette Bradley<br>1980

# Appendix I  Further research: Implications for teaching and remedial work

Since the first edition of this booklet was published, two further research projects have confirmed the young child's skill at detecting rhymes, and how important this is when he learns to read and to spell. Children poor at rhyming who were trained using the remedial techniques described in this booklet were seen to make significant progress in reading and spelling.

**The first project**

The first project was a cross-sectional and longitudinal study designed to answer three questions. The first was to determine whether pre-school children recognise rhymes; evidence to date has been with older children. A second goal was to learn more about alliteration, since a literature search and enquiries among linguists had failed to find any reference to alliteration in discussions on early language development. The third objective was to discover more about the relationship between alliteration, rhyming, reading and spelling.

In this project 64 children were seen, beginning with 16 pre-school children aged 4½, and 16 in each six-month age band up to 6½ years. All the children were tested by Jane Firth, who spent a considerable time with these young children ensuring that they understood what rhyme and alliteration meant in word play and games before testing them. In the first task the children were asked to say a word that (a) rhymed or (b) started the same (alliterative) as a word spoken by the experimenter. There were ten words in each of these two conditions. In the second task the same children were asked to decide whether two words spoken by the experimenter (a) rhymed or (b) were alliterative. Twenty pairs of words were presented in each condition.

The results of this project were quite clear. First of all, pre-school children produce rhymes perfectly well; in fact there was very little change in this skill across the age bands. But there was a clear developmental trend in the young child's ability to recognise rhyme. This improved steadily across the age range. These results help to explain the vast anecdotal literature on the young child's production of rhymes in word play. It is obviously a skill mastered very early on. Rhymes are fun and are a significant part of infant word play. This study shows that children become more adept at recognising rhymes, too, as they grow older.

The answer to our second question was equally clear – there was a striking difference between rhyme and alliteration. There was little response to either the production or recognition alliteration tasks till we came to the children 5½ years of age and older. Then there was a sudden and marked improvement, developmentally significant, in both tasks. Rhymes may be fun but alliterative words are difficult to say. Perhaps it is not suprising that children seem to acquire this skill much later when they have more control over their articulation, and are taught to attend to the beginnings of words in school as they learn to read and to write. Children six-years of age and older do well on the alliteration task; we might say this reflects the child's response to learning. Our earlier research showed that backward readers found the first sound condition particularly difficult.

To find out about the relationship between these skills and reading and spelling the same children were seen in school a year later, and given standardised tests of reading and spelling. Even after the differences in age and vocabulary were taken into account, statistical analysis showed a significant relationship between the children's early skill at production and recognition of both rhyme and alliteration and their scores on the reading and spelling tests. Clearly, young children recognise rhymes before they go to school, and their skill at sound categorisation has a profound effect on their progress in reading and spelling once they get there.

## The second project

We have recently published the results of a second large scale project which not only confirmed the relationship between the young child's early rhyming skill and reading and spelling progress later on, but also showed conclusively that young children who are poor at rhyming when they come to school can be successfully trained to appreciate sound categories and then make good progress in reading and spelling. In this four-year longitudinal project we saw more than 400, four- and five-year old children before they had learned to read or spell. The project fell into two complementary parts, the first being predictive. We gave all the children the 'odd word out' tests of rhyming and alliteration. Because the population was so large we decided to adapt the existing test: we made it easier for the four-year old children and more difficult for the five-year old children, to avoid floor and ceiling effects, and to determine which children would qualify for a controlled training study. As four-year olds have a shorter memory span they were asked the odd word out of three spoken words, in ten trials, in each of three conditions. The five-year olds were asked to detect the odd one out of four spoken words, in ten trials, in each of the three conditions (Test 2); that is, the original test with two extra trials in each condition. In these tasks the child has to remember the words as well as categorise their sounds. To control for this we also gave them 30 memory trials: the child heard the same words and had to recall them straight away. We also tested the children's vocabulary (EPVT) and their IQ(WISC/R) to control for differences in memory, vocabulary and intelligence.

Table 4 (page 38) shows the children's scores on Test 2 at age 5 (and all the children's scores on the same Test 2 at age 8). As the correct response in each trial is the odd word out of four, a score of more than 2.5 out of ten trials is above chance. The scores at age 5, show quite clearly that this is a skill which young children acquire before they learn to read and spell. No child who could read at all was included in the study. Yet on average these five-year olds were correct in 7 out of 10 trials in the rhyming conditions. Their scores on alliteration were lower at age 5. The children had just started school and were not yet so sensitive to the first sound condition. (We can see that this difference between scores in rhyming and alliteration conditions disappeared when the children were older and had been in school longer.)

Three years after the first sound categorisation tests at age 5, when the children were eight- to nine-years old, we gave them all standardised tests of reading and spelling. The results clearly show that children skilled at categorising sounds when they come to school do better at reading and spelling three years later, regardless of intelligence.

**The training study**

The second part of the project was a training study, to ensure that the children's progress was related to their skill at sound categorisation and not some other factor. The 65 children with the lowest scores on the rhyming test were divided into four groups carefully matched on sound categorisation, vocabulary skill and intelligence. Two groups were given training in sound categorisation using the *Sound Pictures* cards (for example, putting the picture for hen, men, pen together). One of these groups also made the words with the plastic letters, as recommended in the 'Remediation' section, for half the sessions. The other two groups were a control. One control group was also trained using the *Sound Pictures* cards but was taught to group them on the basis of meaning (hen, dog, cat are animals), while the second control group continued their usual class lessons but received no special training. The children were seen individually for 40, ten-minute sessions over two years.

At the end of the project the children were given standardised tests of reading and spelling. The children trained to categorise sounds were consistently three to four months ahead of the control children who were trained to categorise the same words semantically. The children who were trained with the alphabetic letters as well as *Sound Pictures* were reading ten months ahead of the trained control group and fourteen months ahead of the children who received no training. Their spelling scores were seventeen months in advance of the trained control group and twenty-three months ahead of the untrained children. Our obvious conclusion must be that even short training sessions on sound categorisation, using these methods, have a significant effect.

Taken together, the results of the longitudinal and training studies provide conclusive evidence that the child's awareness of rhyme and alliteration has a powerful influence on his eventual success in reading and spelling.

Rhyming is a natural way of learning to generalise from one spoken word to another, and it is a natural way to learn to segment the syllable. Both skills are essential if we are to learn to read and to spell. We need to be able to generalise from one word to another so that each word we meet is not unique. If words had nothing in common the number we could learn would be very limited. To work out a word we cannot spell or read, generalising from a word we do know, we need to be able to use the alphabet. To use the alphabet we have to be able to segment speech units, and rhyming is the natural way to learn this too, because words only rhyme if they are identical from their stressed vowel onwards. 'City' and 'duty' are the same at the end, but they do not rhyme. 'Duty' and 'beauty' rhyme, and so do 'hen' and 'pen'. The natural analysis when we rhyme or use alliteration takes place within the syllabic unit.

So when little children play with words, and distort them to make them rhyme, they are learning to analyse speech units in the most natural way possible. It is not surprising that those children who have mastered these skills in word play before they come to school, learn to read and spell more easily.

# Appendix II   Norms for the sound categorisation tests

*Table 3*
Scores on Test 1 and details of a sample of 83 young children selected because they were in the early stages of learning to read and to spell.

|  | Mean | S.D. | Range Minimum | Maximum |
|---|---|---|---|---|
|  | No. Correct out of 8 |  |  |  |
| First Sound | 5.30 | 1.93 | 0 | 8 |
| Middle Sound | 5.26 | 1.82 | 2 | 8 |
| Last Sound | 5.20 | 1.69 | 1 | 8 |
|  | Months |  |  |  |
| Chronological Age | 76.72 | 5.25 | 63 | 86 |
| Schonell R.A. | 77.45 | 4.34 | 72 | 96 |
| Schonell Spelling | 65.69 | 6.20 | 60 | 85 |

*Table 4*
Scores on Test 2 for 264 children at age 5, (non-readers), and for 368 children at age 8.

Mean No. Correct out of 10+

|  | 5 Years Mean No. Correct | S.D. | 8 Years Mean No. Correct | S.D. |
|---|---|---|---|---|
| First Sound | 5.36 | 2.29 | 8.79 | 1.63 |
| Middle Sound | 6.89 | 2.35 | 8.68 | 1.73 |
| Last Sound | 6.67 | 2.33 | 8.97 | 1.61 |

+ a score above 2.5 is above chance level

|  | Months |  | Months |  |
|---|---|---|---|---|
| Chronological Age | 65 | 3.8 | 101.54 | 4.21 |
| Schonell R.A. | — | — | 100.91 | 16.64 |
| Schonell Spelling Age | — | — | 94.88 | 17.58 |

Name _____ birth date _____ age _____ test date _____
nursery rhyme _____ speech _____
language _____ comments _____

## Condition 1

*First sound different*

| | | | | | | | | |
|---|---|---|---|---|---|---|---|---|
| rot | rod | rock | box | | | | | |
| lick | lid | miss | lip | | | | | |

| bud | bun | bus | rug |
| pip | pin | hill | pig |
| ham | tap | had | hat |
| peg | pen | well | pet |
| kid | kick | kiss | fill |
| lot | mop | lock | log |
| leap | mean | meal | meat |
| crack | crab | crag | trap |
| slim | flip | slick | slip |
| roof | room | food | root |

*Errors* _____

## Condition 2

*Last sound different*

| fan | cat | hat | mat |
| leg | peg | hen | beg |

| pin | win | sit | fin |
| bun | doll | hop | top | pop |
| bun | bun | hut | gun | sun |
| peg | map | cap | gap | pal |
| kid | men | red | bed | fed |
| wig | fig | pin | dig |
| weed | peel | need | deed |
| pack | lack | sad | back |
| sand | hand | land | bank |
| sink | mint | pink | wink |

*Errors* _____

## Condition 3

*Middle sound different*

| mop | hop | tap | lop |
| pat | bat | fit | cat |

| lot | cot | pot | hat |
| fun | pin | bun | gun |
| hug | dig | pig | wig |
| red | fed | lid | bed |
| wag | rag | bag | leg |
| fell | doll | well | bell |
| man | bin | pin | tin |
| fog | dog | mug | log |
| feed | need | wood | seed |
| fish | dish | wish | mash |

*Errors* _____

Notes

# References

1. Goodacre, E., 1979, 'What is reading: Which model', Raggett, M., Tutt,C., Taggett,P. (eds.) *Assessment and Testing of Reading: Problems and Practices* (London: Ward Lock Educational)

2. Naidoo, S., 1972, *Specific Dyslexia* (London: Pitman)

3. Mattis, S., French, J. and Rapin, I., 1975, 'Dyslexia in children and young adults: three independent neuropsychological syndromes', *Developmental Medicine and Child Neurology, 17,* 150-163

4. Boder, E., 1973, Developmental dyslexia: a diagnostic approach based on 3 atypical reading-spelling patterns, *Developmental Medicine and Child Neurology, 15,* 663

5. Raggett, P., 1979, 'Ongoing Assessment in the Classroom', Raggett, M., Tutt,C., Raggett,P. (eds.) *Assessment and Testing of Reading: Problems and Practices* (London: Ward Lock Educational)

6. Shankweiler, D., 1964, 'Developmental Dyslexia: a critique and review of recent evidence', *Cortex, 1,* 53-62

7. Bradley, L., 1980, 'Reading, Writing and Spelling Problems', Gordon, N., McInlay, I. (eds.) *Helping Clumsy Children* (Edinburgh: Churchill Livingstone)

8. Goodacre, E., 1967, *Reading in Infant Classes: A survey of the Teaching Practice and Conditions in 100 schools and Departments.* (Slough, Bucks: N.F.E.R.)

9. Donaldson, M., 1978, *Children's Minds* (Glasgow: Fontana)

10. Gibson, E., Levin, H., 1975, *The Psychology of Reading,* (Cambridge, Mass.: M.I.T.)

11. Smith, F., 1971, *Understanding Reading* (New York: Holt, Rinehart & Winston)

12  Steinberg, D., Yamada, J., 1979, *'Are whole word kanji easier to learn than syllable kana?* Reading Research Quarterly. *1,* 88-99

13  Barron R., Baron, J., 1977, 'How children get meaning from printed words', *Child Development, 48,* 587-594

14  Bradley, L., Hulme C., Bryant P., 1979, 'The connexion between different verbal difficulties in a backward reader: a case study', *Developmental Medicine and Child Neurology.*

15  Jansky, J., de Hirsch, K., 1972, *Preventing Reading Failure* (New York: Harper & Row)

16  Baron, J., 1978, 'The Word Superiority Effect: perceptual learning from reading', Estes, W.K. (ed.) *Handbook of Learning and Cognitive Processes,* vol. 6 (L.E.A.)

17  Bradley, L., 1979, 'Visual memory and Cross-modal connexions in Reading and Spelling', Ph.D. thesis

18  Bradley, L., 1979, 'The Discovery that Backward Readers have difficulty Copying', Ph.D. thesis

19  Rosen, C., 1966, 'An experimental study of visual perceptual training and reading achievement in first grade' *Percept. Motor Skills, 22,* 979

20  Beck, R., Talkington, L., 1970, 'Frostig training with Head Start Children', *Percept. Motor Skills, 30,* 521

21  Gorelick, M., 1965, 'The effectiveness of visual form training in a pre-reading program', *Journal of Educational Research, 58,* 315

22  Bradley, L., Bryant, P., 1978, 'Difficulties in auditory organisation as a possible cause of reading backwardness' *Nature, 271,* 746

23  Conrad, R., 1972, 'Speech and Reading', Kavanagh, J., Mattingly, I. (eds.) *Language by Ear and by Eye: the Relationships between Speech and Reading* (Cambridge, Mass.: M.I.T. Press)

24  Conrad, R., 1977, 'The Reading Ability of Deaf School Leavers', *Brit. J. Ed. Psych., 47,* 2, 138-148

25  Johnson, D., Myklebust, H., 1967, *Learning Disabilities* (New York: Grune and Stratton)

26  Myklebust, H., 1965, *Development and Disorders of Written Language* (New York: Grune and Stratton)

27  Myklebust, H., 1960, *The Psychology of Deafness* (New York: Grune and Stratton)

28  Tansley, A., 1967, *Reading and Remedial Reading* (London: Routledge & Kegan Paul)

29  Vellutino, F., Steger, J. and Kandel, G., 1972, 'Reading disability: an investigation of the perceptual deficit hypothesis', *Cortex, 8,* 106-118

30  Clark, M.M., 1970, *Reading Difficulties in Schools* (Harmondsworth: Penguin)

31  Wepman, J., 1960, 'Auditory discrimination, speech and reading', *Elementary School Journal, 60,* 325-333

32  de Hirsch, K., Jansky, J. and Langford, W., 1966, *Predicting Reading Failure* (New York: Harper & Row)

33  Blank, M., 1968, 'Cognitive Processes in Auditory Discrimination in Normal and Retarded Readers', *Child Development, 39,* 4,1091

34  Savin, H., 1972, 'What the child knows about speech when he starts to learn to read', Kavanagh, J. and Mattingley, I. (eds.) *Language by Ear and by Eye: the Relationships between Speech and Reading* (Cambridge, Mass.: M.I.T. Press) pp. 319-327

35  Liberman, I., Shankweiler, D., Fischer, F. and Carter B., 1974, 'Reading and the awareness of linguistic segments', *Journal of Experimental Psychology, 18,* 201-212

36  Liberman, I., Shankweiler, D., Liberman, A., Fowler, C. and Fischer, F., 1977, 'Phonetic segmentation and recoding in the beginning reader', Reber, A. and Scarborough, D. (eds.) *Toward a Psychology of Reading* (New Jersey: Laurence Erlbaum Associates) pp. 207-226

37  Liberman I., 1973, 'Segmentation of the spoken word and reading acquisition', *Bulletin of the Orton Society, 23,* 65-77

38  Rozin, P., Gleitman, L., 1977, 'The structure and acquisition of reading, II: the reading process and the acquisition of the alphabetic principle', Reber, A. and Scarborough, D. (eds.) *Toward a Psychology of Reading* (New Jersey: Laurence Erlbaum Associates) pp. 55-142

39  Warren, R., 1972, 'Temporal resolution of auditory events'. Paper presented at American Psychological Association (Honolulu, Hawaii)

40  Warren, R., 1976, 'Auditory Perception and Speech Evolution', *Annals of the New York Academy of Sciences, 280,* 708-717

41  Chukovsky, K., 1956, quoted in Elkonin, D., 1971, 'Development of Speech' in Zaporozhets, A., Elkonin, D. (eds.), 1971, *The Psychology of Pre-school Children* (Cambridge, Mass.: M.I.T. Press)

42  Bullock, A., 1975, *'A Language for Life',* Report of the Committee of Inquiry appointed by the Secretary of State for Education and Science (London: H.M.S.O.)

43  Jordan, D., 1972, *Dyslexia in the Classroom* (Columbus Ohio: Merill)

44  Bradley, L., 1979, 'Difficulties in Auditory Organisation as a Possible Cause of Reading Backwardness', *Perceptual and Cognitive Difficulties Experienced by Able Backward Readers* (Unpublished Ph.D. thesis)

45  Bradley, L., Bryant, P., 1979, 'Independence of Reading and Spelling in Backward and Normal Readers', *Developmental Medicine and Child Neurology, 21,* 504-514

46 Cotterell, G., 1970, 'Teaching Procedures' in Franklin A., Naidoo S. (eds.) *Assessment and teaching of dyslexic children* (London: I.C.A.A.)

47 Gillingham, A., Stillman B., 1977, *Remedial training for children with specific difficulty in reading, spelling and penmanship*, 7th ed. (Cambridge, Mass.: Educators Publishing Service)

48 Bradley, L., Bryant, P., 1983, 'Categorising sounds and learning to read: a causal connexion', *Nature, 301*, 419–421

# Further publications

Bradley, L., 1981, 'The Organisation of Motor Patterns for Spelling: an effective remedial strategy for backward readers', *Developmental Medicine and Child Neurology, 23,* 83-91

Bradley, L. and Bryant, P., 1981, 'Visual Memory and Phonological Skills in Reading and Spelling Backwardness', *Psychological Research, 43,* 193-199

Bradley, L., 1981, *Sound Pictures*, Macmillan Education

Bradley, L., 1982, 'Alliteration, rhyming, reading and spelling in young children and backward readers. Abstracts B.P.S. London Conference', *Bulletin of the British Psychological Society, 35,* 18

Bradley, L. and Bryant, P., 1983, 'Categorising Sounds and Learning to Read: a causal connexion', *Nature, 301,* 419-421

Bradley, L., 1983, 'The Organisation of Visual, Phonological and Motor Strategies in Reading and Spelling', Kirk, U. (ed.), *Neuropsychology of Language, Reading and Spelling,* New York: Academic Press